Ten of the Best Ne
Trout Flies

Ten of the Best New Zealand Trout Flies

Where and when to use them and how to tie them

Mike Weddell

JOHN McINDOE

line drawings   Patricia Altman

ISBN 0 86868 0974

*First published and printed 1987 by
John McIndoe Limited, 51 Crawford Street,
Dunedin, New Zealand*

Cover: *A splendid brown taken from the Brightwater, a small stream in
northern Southland. Nearly 4kg in weight, it was caught on a Hare's Ear
Nymph.*   (Photo Sue Weddell)

CONTENTS

(Colour illustrations between pp. 32 & 33)

FIRST STEPS TOWARDS SUCCESS

Over the twenty-three years that I have been a fly fisher I have been fortunate enough to meet many such anglers and of these a few have stood, figuratively speaking, head and shoulders above the rest. This elite band didn't fish and hope to catch fish, they fished and caught fish. What made them more successful than their contemporaries, in whichever country they fished or branch of the sport in which they specialised, was that they all had several qualities in common. All were acutely observant, all constantly strove to improve their knowledge both of trout and their ways, all were persistent rather than patient, and regardless of their profession all were first and foremost fly fishers.

I learned a lot from all of them, but probably the most important thing I learnt was that if I wished to catch fish consistently I had to understand the feeding patterns of trout and be familiar with the creatures on which trout fed. When these fly fishers tied on flies they knew what they represented and they knew how to make the flies act like the real thing. Their fly boxes weren't full of fancy flies that were products of some misguided imagination, each fly in the box represented something in nature to them and, more importantly, to the trout.

There are literally thousands of trout fly patterns many of which I call, perhaps unkindly, folklore flies. These flies have been arrived at by trial and error, by ringing the changes of colour, size and shape until eventually fish are caught more or less consistently with them. The logical approach is to observe the creatures on which trout feed and then specifically set out to tie an imitation of that creature. But that is only half the story. To deceive fish consistently anglers should also make their specific imitations mimic the actions of this or that live creature.

Fly fishers have usually shown allegiance to either of two schools of thought on how to catch trout. One school advocates as exact an imitation as possible, the other places priority on mimicking the actions of the trout's food. To these anglers presentation is all important. Presentation is a term bandied around in angling circles but it is rarely defined. It simply means making your fly behave as if it were the live creature that it imitates in form and colour. Now I think most intelligent anglers would agree that the wisest policy is to adopt the best from both schools of thought. Tie the best possible imitation and combine that with as near perfect presentation as possible. Once you accept this argument you are well on your way to becoming a consistently successful fly fisher.

I want to briefly recount some experiences that testify to the importance of both imitation and presentation. On one occasion I was fishing Rutland Water in the English Midlands. I was in the middle of a purple patch, fishing two or three evenings a week to rainbows rising to hatching midge pupae. A midge pupa imitation in size 12 and 14 consistently caught fish until one evening, with a light breeze gently rippling the water, the rainbows started to rise in big numbers. I covered fish after fish without so much as a hint of interest from the trout. Two brothers that I regularly encountered at Rutland were fishing not far away and they weren't having any success either. The fish were rising frequently. Sometimes individual fish were rising two or three times while travelling no more than two metres. I did all the right things for cruising rainbows, casting well in front as rainbows usually cruise quickly, and slowly retrieved the flies to imitate midge pupae on their way to the surface to hatch. Then it suddenly dawned on me that these rainbows must be cruising very close to the surface if they are rising so frequently, and that by casting well ahead I was probably allowing my flies to sink below the fish. From experience I knew that trout hardly, if ever, picked up food that was below them in the water and that in the poor light of that evening they probably couldn't see the flies. I greased my leader and the team of three midge pupae imitations I was fishing to keep them right on the surface. The first fish I cast to took without hesitation and was soon on the bank. After I'd landed another I passed the message on to my neighbours and they were soon playing fish too. In the next hour we landed more than a dozen rainbows between us, the fish averaging just under a kilo. The fish were still rising when we had to drag ourselves away at the official finishing time, one hour after sunset.

There is much debate over the importance of colour in trout flies. Some say the colour is absolutely critical; others say it is of no importance whatsoever. As usual with such polarised views the answer probably lies somewhere between the two. I lean towards the importance of colour as a result of another experience on Rutland Water — coincidently the same two brothers were again fishing close by that evening. Few fish were rising and those were miles out of range. As the sun set the rises began to get closer. I was fishing my usual team of flies; a Black Midge Pupa on the top dropper, a Green Midge Pupa in the middle, and a Cove Pheasant Tail Nymph as the end fly. Most of my fish on Rutland were rainbows caught on the Cove Nymph which is a very good midge pupae imitation. The first fish that rose within range that evening took one of my flies, but after a short run and jump it threw the hook. The second wasn't so fortunate. On landing it I found it had taken the Green Pupa. I jokingly called to my companions that this fish had made a mistake and taken the Green Pupa instead of the Cove Nymph. By the time I started casting again several fish were rising and a second took hold of one of my flies. Again it was the Green Pupa. I told the others and asked them if they had a Green Pupa imitation. One of them had and tied it on; the other hadn't so I gave him one of mine. By the time he'd tied it on his brother had hooked a fish on his first cast. Brother number two hooked a fish first cast too, but it broke the line after a run and jump. By this time we had to leave as it was an hour after sunset. We were very conscientious, especially as the ranger was sitting in his landrover watching us.

There are many other examples I could relate of how colour and presentation is critical, but the two instances described are good examples as they concern the same insect being imitated under similar conditions. An equally important factor in successfully deceiving trout is the size of the fly used. As an example of what I mean here is a tale of an outing on some superb water nearer to home.

I was on the Clutha just below the outlet of Lake Wanaka. It was towards the end of March, the weather was clear, warm and calm, and the spinners fell by the million. I'd only ever heard of the famous sedge rise at the outlet of the lake and this spinner fall took me by surprise. On the gravel beach at the outlet itself the spent spinners were washed ashore in heaps; it was possible to scoop up hundreds in one handful. Several fish were sipping spinners from the surface but too far out to reach. I walked downstream on the Wanaka side of the river and found several fish feeding within casting distance. I waded out carefully in the gin clear water and took up position below the nearest fish. I could see every detail of the fish as it swung from side to side picking spinners from the surface. Strong positive rises as the trout slurped down the live spinners. There were fewer spinners than at the outlet and the fish took virtually every one that drifted down. I had already tied on my standard spinner imitation. I lengthened line and dropped the fly a metre above and half a metre to the left of the fish. The trout swung across to intercept my offering but to my disbelief turned away at the last minute. The same thing happened on the next cast, then the trout totally ignored the fly on subsequent casts.

Something was wrong. I caught a spinner as it drifted past and held my imitation alongside it. The colour of the body was a good match and the hackle seemed a fair representation of wings and legs. But the anomaly was the length of the body. The natural was between 1 and 2mm shorter in the body than my fly. My fly was too big, not by much, but that had to be the deciding factor as my imitation had accounted for many fish feeding on deleatidium spinners in the past.

The size 14 I was fishing was the smallest I had with me so I was stuck for the moment. Being ever optimistic I tried for another fish but with the same result before the rise petered out. That evening I tied up several size 16 spinners. The next morning spinners were again sailing down the Clutha and I located a good fish rising to them. It was a long way off and moving about a lot but eventually I was able to sail the fly over the trout without drag and it took without hesitation. After several minutes of too-ing and fro-ing I landed the fish with the tiny fly securely fastened to the corner of his jaw. The trout was about 2kg and since it had served the purpose of my experiment I released it. The next two fish I found within range were equally obliging and reinforced the importance of size when selecting an imitation.

I have already mentioned that there are thousands of different trout fly patterns, which makes the selection of the correct pattern on any given day a daunting task, especially for the beginner. *But once it is realised that the number of creatures that make up the bulk of trout diet are probably no more than a dozen, the problem of fly selection is brought down to manageable proportions.* A single good imitation of each creature at each stage of the creature's development is all that is needed to produce the goods, i.e. catch trout!

From the argument presented in this chapter it may seem contradictory that subsequent chapters are devoted to particular fly patterns and not to individual creatures that form trout diet. Ultimately the angler has to decide what fly to use, and dealing with individual patterns and relating them to the world of the trout, rather than the other way round, is an attempt to simplify what can be a complex process of deduction. The patterns described imitate specific food forms and their success has been evaluated. They work.

NOTE

Although the examples I've used to show where, when and how to fish the flies covered in this book are drawn from my experience in the south of the South Island (simply because I live in Otago), the techniques are equally applicable throughout New Zealand, and also in a great many other countries where trout are caught on fly. In New Zealand, I've used the flies successfully in the Taupo-Rotorua district, the Wairarapa and around Blenheim. Wherever you go the bulk of trout food is based on relatively few food forms, consequently the basic techniques described in this book translate well from region to region, and country to country. In other words, these flies and these methods will catch trout wherever you fish.

M.W.

THE PATTERNS

BLACK AND PEACOCK

It was a cold grey morning with a fitful breeze ruffling patches of the surface of Lake Wanaka. There had been a dusting of snow on the hills overnight — hardly promising conditions for fishing Paddock Bay. Having fished the bay for the previous four mornings I was in no hurry to get a fly on to the water until I'd seen a fish move. Besides I was in plenty of time; it was just after 7 a.m. and the best of the fishing had been from 8-10 a.m.

There was no sign of a midge rise, there weren't even any adult midge in the air, and as I walked slowly through the shallows only a few waterboatmen darted off to safety. There were, however, lots of water snails on the bottom and clinging to twigs and fronds of weed. Since snails formed the most readily available source of food for the local trout it seemed sensible to fish a snail imitation, the good old Black and Peacock Spider (B & P). As simple a fly as you could wish for if you tie your own, a simplicity matched by its trout catching qualities on the right day.

My imitation was tied on a size 14 hook and my tippet was 2.8kg breaking strain. The water was fairly clear and I'd have picked a finer tippet but for the weed and the size of the fish. On my first visit to Paddock Bay I'd hooked fifteen fish on the B & P, but three of the first half dozen had broken the tippet by running straight out into deep water, then turning through ninety degrees and dragging twenty-five metres of fly line and several metres of backing through the plentiful weedbeds until the strain was too great. A step up in tippet size prevented any more breaks.

But it's no consolation knowing you've got the right fly and your tippet is strong enough, if you can't find a fish to cast at. I prefer to fish the B & P in flat calm conditions as fish that are snailing can often be spotted cruising the shallows. If the water is shallow enough, or the fish is big enough, its tail may break the surface of the water as it picks a snail from the lake bed. Snails don't move very quickly and consequently the trout feeding on them, realising the snails can't get away from them, move slowly too. This is an advantage from the angler's point of view, for if he sees a tail or dorsal fin break the surface and gets his fly into the area fairly quickly, there's a fair chance the fish will still be close enough to see the fly.

The wind dropped and the ripple disappeared from an area of shallows in front of me, so I waded slowly through the weedbeds about thirty metres from shore. A fish moved well ahead and a few seconds later its tail broke the surface again. I waded a little quicker but still kept my eyes open for any fish that might be between me and the one moving for the third time about fifty metres away. As I walked I lengthened line but cast away to the right so as not to scare any fish I hadn't yet spotted. Another fish moved to my left between me and the shore and well within casting distance. By the time I had my fly in front of it, the fish had 'risen' several times more. Either the fish didn't see the fly or it didn't like the pattern for the trout swam straight past the fly. Next time I dropped the B & P very close to the fish so it had to see the splash as the fly hit the water. The tippet slowly drew under as the fly sank, then suddenly the leader began to draw to the right. I tightened and the fish rolled on the surface. I backed off and led it away from the first fish I'd spotted so I'd still have a chance of catching it. The fish played hard, as fish hooked in shallow water usually do, making several dashes towards deeper water. Gradually the trout tired and I ran it on to a sandy spit and picked it up.

A nice fish of 1.5kg with mainly snails in its gut and a few water-boatmen. While I was gutting this fish the wind began to ripple the water again. I stood on the shore examining the water where the other fish had been rising. Nothing, not a sign. I waded slowly out and to the right with the wind at my back. I was surprised at how well I could see into the water with both the wind and light behind me. I worked a length of line out on to the water just in case and continued wading slowly down wind. After a few minutes I spotted a fish cruising quite quickly from left to right. I dropped the B & P about a metre in front of it. The fish accelerated and its mouth opened as it reached the spot. The trout made a dash for open water but I must have tightened a little too quickly for after about ten metres the hook pulled out.

It began to drizzle and the light was poor, but it was too early to pack up so I stood on the shore watching for any tell-tale movement. Some days the wind begins to blow and gets stronger as the day goes on; other days it comes and goes. Luckily this was one of the latter days. After about fifteen minutes patches of calm began to appear well out from the shore. I waded out to the nearest calm patch in the middle of which was the remnant of a mai mai from last shooting season. As I approached the mai mai a trout cruised out from behind it and headed straight towards me. I flicked the rod and the fly dropped right in front of the fish and was picked up without hesitation. That one didn't drop off even though it was a long wade back to shore to beach the fish. This was bigger than the first fish but not in such good condition. I put it back.

The wind was up again and the calm patches were disappearing. The best prospect looked to be over where a line of willows ran out into the lake.

I saw two fish move once each as I made my way to the willows, then nothing for a while. The wind was gradually increasing and my calm patch was shrinking rapidly. A fish moved between me and the willows. I covered the spot, casting slightly to the right as I guessed that was the direction in which the trout was moving. No response. It moved again closer to the willows. Again I covered the fish; again no response. For a third time the trout moved, plainly travelling from left to right. This time I cast well in front of it. A steady pull took the leader under and I struck. I worked the fish clear of the willows and despite picking up a couple of bunches of weed on the line I played the trout out and picked it up where I stood to save the 300 metre round trip to the shore. A 2kg fish this time and in good condition too.

I might as well have walked the fish to the shore as it started to rain and the wind really began to blow, but it was nearly breakfast time anyway. Not the best morning's sport ever, but turning four chances into three landed fish was quite satisfying.

Although I usually prefer to fish with the B & P either casting to fish cruising the bottom, or foraging in the weedbeds, I've often had success fishing it blind. I usually use a larger size than when fishing visually, a ten or a twelve. Ideal conditions for fishing the B & P blind is when the water is choppy and there are weedbeds in the area. The wave action often washes the snails off the weed and carries them out into open water. So the tactic is to fish on the downwind side of a weedbed, casting out and just letting the fly

14

carry round in the ripple as if fishing in flowing water. No retrieve is really necessary as the line is kept tight by the drift. Some fly fishers are habitual retrievers and find it difficult to let things just drift, so if you are one of these, retrieve as slowly as possible. A couple of centimetres every second would be fast enough. Remember the artificial should imitate the natural in action not just in looks.

When trout are especially jumpy the B & P can be used to good effect when a fish is spotted cruising a regular beat. When the fish is well out of range cast the fly so that it sinks to the bottom in such a position that the fish will swim close by it. Quite often a fish will pick it up without further inducement. However, if the trout looks like ignoring it, give the fly a little twitch so that it moves a couple of centimetres along the bottom. That usually does the trick and the fish will pounce on it.

The snail is more often thought of as a food of stillwater trout, or the French, but there are occasions when trout in streams and rivers will feed on snails. I've had good catches of fish that had been feeding exclusively on snails. In such circumstances the B & P is fished dead drift just as any nymph would be fished in running water.

Although it is a good snail imitation, the B & P is also a reasonable representation of other food forms. On one occasion it provided the answer to two Mataura fish that refused all previous offerings although they continued feeding. I'd already caught several fish on a Hare's Ear Nymph but the nearest fish didn't even look at it. Some of the fish I'd caught earlier had had willow grub in them so I gave that a try. No response. All the time I was trying for this fish I was scanning the surface of the water for a clue as to what the trout was taking. After I'd been trying for a while I spotted a tiny black beetle drifting by, then a couple more. It was worth a chance. I tied on a size 16 B & P. The fish took it first cast. There were several of the black beetles in its gut, as well as some tiny green leaf bugs. The second fish was equally obliging. Unfortunately as this one took the fly it turned towards me and I only managed to feel the weight of the trout before the hook came away. However, it was a lesson to remember.

There is one occasion when the B & P may hold the key to success but often it is not recognised. Snails can float and at times on still-waters they can be seen by the thousands bobbing up and down in the ripples. When trout take these floating snails they disturb the surface creating a rise form which resembles that produced when trout rise to midge pupae or other surface food. If you are getting no response to other patterns try a B & P if snails are floating about. It needs to be fished on or very close to the surface. This can be accomplished by greasing the leader to within 2-3 centimetres of the fly. When taking surface food trout look up. Anything that is below them in the water is ignored, so the fly must be where they are looking.

You will find many of the snails that trout feed on are quite small, as small as 3-4 millimetres. Now if normal practice were followed, an imitation would be tied on a very small hook which would decrease the chances of landing big fish. There is a simple solution — tie a life size imitation on a large hook. The body is tied to cover only the part of the hook shank nearest the eye. The trout don't seem to mind the hook sticking out behind.

Snails are to be found in waters all over the south from Te Anau to the Taieri and from Benmore to Tomahawk lagoons. They are always available for trout to feed on and they often do. So make sure you always have a B & P to hand just in case.

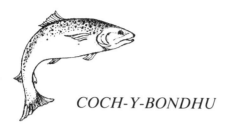

COCH-Y-BONDHU

Beetles form an important if irregular part of the diet of trout and it would be an unwise fly fisher that ventured out on to any New Zealand water without a suitable imitation in his fly box. Beetles come in all shapes and sizes, but probably those of most importance to the trout and the fly fisher are the brown beetle and the manuka beetle.

Fishing the 'cochy' conjures up in my mind's eye the clear blue skies and golden hills of Central Otago in high summer. But that is not the whole picture by any means. I have found brown beetles in the back garden in June and have caught fish on the 'Cochy' in every month of the season from November till April, and I'm sure the only reason I haven't caught one in October is because I haven't tried it. Also the biggest swarms of beetles (if that is the collective noun for beetles) I've seen were on the lower Taieri at Outram, and on Knights Dam above Lake Mahinerangi. On both occasions there were millions of them in the air just on dark, yet surprisingly the best fishing I've had with the 'Cochy' has been when relatively few beetles were in evidence. But that doesn't mean to say they weren't there.

I remember meeting up with a very obliging rainbow on the Upper Ahuriri a few years ago. It was a hot day and I'd walked a long way without seeing a single fish. I spotted a nice looking backwater on the far side of the river. I managed to wade across although the water was almost up to my armpits. Where the current swirled and eddied at the entrance to the backwater a fish rose, then a short distance away was another rise, then another. The water was clear but the angle of the light prevented me from seeing how many fish were there. At the downstream side of the backwater was a steep bank more than 10 metres above the water, an ideal position to take a look at the fish. Once I was up there, all was revealed. A rainbow was moving back and forward and from side to side over a considerable area. The fish rose every half minute or so. With such a vantage point I took the opportunity of photographing the rising fish. This took several minutes, but the fish rose relentlessly. Eventually I climbed down to water level and looked on and into the water for a clue as to what the fish might be taking. There didn't appear to be anything for the trout to be feeding on at all, never mind enough of whatever it was to totally occupy him.

When in doubt, tie on a 'Cochy', and that is what I did. I still couldn't see the fish in the water, only his scattered rises helped locate him. It took a few attempts to synchronise the positions of the fly and the fish but he took as soon as he spotted it. When I'd played and landed the fish I could hardly contain my curiosity to see what the rainbow had been taking. It was full, and I mean full, of green beetles, hundreds of them. No wonder he was keen to take the 'Cochy'.

Since then the 'Cochy' has become my favourite dry fly for exploring the water, especially in back country waters. The method of using the 'Cochy' for exploring the water is exactly the same as when using a nymph for the same purpose. All the fishy looking water is covered once or twice. Repetitive casting doesn't usually work. If the fish are on they usually take first time over. The obvious place for fish to lie and wait for terrestrial insects such as beetles or cicadas is close to the bank, especially if the bank is undercut with thick vegetation that harbours these insects. The insects often fall in the water and the trout are there waiting.

A good way of methodically exploring smaller back country streams is to wade slowly upstream placing one cast close to the left hand bank, one cast in the middle and one cast against the right bank, this way most fish in the water will be covered by the fly. The more trout that see the fly the better the chances of finding a fish looking for a beetle or two. In such waters there is rarely enough of any particular food form to keep trout preoccupied and they are opportunistic feeders. Provided they don't have to expend too much energy to get to it they'll have a go at most morsels coming their way. The 'Cochy' fits the bill as it is a solid looking mouthful and highly visible to the fish. Equally important it floats well in rough water and is readily seen by the angler.

It is quite common to have a back country day where every rise you see is to the 'Cochy' at the end of your leader. In fact I'd be tempted to state that only two flies are needed to fish back country streams, a nymph and of course the 'Cochy'. However, there are always exceptional occasions when neither will work and it's nice to have the comfort of a few back up patterns.

Despite not being an infallible fly, the 'Cochy' will often produce the goods when others fail. I remember yet another occasion on the Ahuriri finding a good fish in a slowly rotating backwater. The fish was facing towards me as I approached from downstream and was just under the surface. I crouched down as soon as I spotted the trout and hoped it hadn't seen me. The fish rose a couple of times as I watched. I had a nymph on, having just fished a ripple, so I thought I'd give it a try. The nymph plopped into the water a metre or so from the fish which moved straight towards it, but turned away at the last minute. (Fish in bright sunny weather, especially when close to the surface, can be very spooky and it doesn't pay to cast too close. Besides they can see a long way and will often move a considerable distance to take or inspect a fly.) I dropped the nymph a little closer on the next cast and the fish didn't even look at it. I retreated from the water's edge and replaced the nymph with a size 12 'Cochy', large enough I thought in such bright clear conditions, although when exploring I wouldn't hesitate to use a size 10.

Creeping back into position I lengthened line and dropped the 'Cochy' on the water rather short, but the fish moved straight over and took it without hesitation. After a hard fight I had a fish of over 3kg on the bank. There wasn't much in the trout's stomach, a few blow flies and the odd beetle, but the 'Cochy' is a good imitation of both. Coincidentally I caught another fish of the same weight from the same spot in a similar manner a year later.

Of course, a 'Cochy' should be fished dead drift, just like an insect being washed along helplessly, but not always. On the upper Taieri I found a nice fish feeding under the shade of a willow. The 'Cochy' drifted over the trout the first time and it moved up to the fly almost balancing it on its nose. The fish dropped back a couple of metres in this position then headed back to its lie. It was a difficult position in which to cast so I began to pull in line, skating the fly across the surface. The fish turned and in a flash had taken the fly and was landed. You never can tell!

So far I've only mentioned using the 'Cochy' in running water, but it can be used with equal success on stillwater. I've found the 'Cochy' will catch fish feeding on cicadas and damsel flies, two insects I'm sure the 'Cochy's' anonymous Welsh inventor never intended it to imitate.

Most summers' days cicadas can be heard chirping around Lake Mahinerangi but for some obscure reason (obscure to me, but maybe not to others) they do not often find their way on to the water. Even under apparently identical conditions, one day will see the water covered with cicadas struggling and kicking, yet another day not a one will ripple the surface. On the other hand, I've seen masses of cicadas on the water on bright breezy days and on dull calm days. The only apparent common factor that seems to inspire cicadas to go for a swim is the temperature. It must be warm.

When the cicadas become water-borne the trout are quick to take advantage of their meals on wings. As the cicadas bob along in the ripple the trout work up wind picking them off as they go. A size 10 'Cochy' cast slightly upwind and allowed to drift in the area where fish are rising does the trick. Again the fly is visible even in the peaty waters of Mahinerangi. The fly has a strong silhouette and the trout are cruising close to the surface looking for food above and can't fail to see it. At such times activity can be intense with trout rising everywhere, so the temptation is to cast to every rise. Don't! More success will be had by casting among the rises and leaving the fly to drift. In my experience fish travel quickly when feeding on cicadas and will veer from side to side some considerable distance to pick one up. If you cast to a rise the chances are the fly will be behind or to one side of the fish and it won't be seen. Falls of cicadas usually occur during the middle of the day and start and stop suddenly. You can never tell how long the activity will last so you've got to make the most of it.

A Coch-y-bondhu doesn't look much like a damsel fly, but for some reason trout will often — but not always — take a 'Cochy' when feeding on damsel flies. I have caught trout on Lake Benmore that have been stuffed full of red damsel flies. The fish jump clear of the water to capture these insects as they hover a few centimetres above the surface of the lake. Despite this they readily take a 'Cochy' sitting motionless on the water.

It is tempting to assume that the Coch-y-bondhu is the dry fly for all occasions. It definitely is not the fly for all occasions, just most of them.

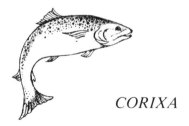

CORIXA

Whenever I think of fishing the Waterboatman (or Corixa) my mind conjures up the scene of a flat calm lagoon on a clear, cold morning. The sun is just peeping over the eastern hills bathing the valley in golden light. The background chatter of waterfowl is punctuated by the 'clicking' of pied stilts wading the margins and the spur-winged plovers raucously protest when you approach too close. Then there is a swirl close to the weedbed at the near end of the lagoon and before the spreading rings have disappeared another fish moves further out.

The temptation is to rush to the water's edge and get the fly into the water as quickly as possible. But such haste can be counter-productive even though there is no question about which fly to use. With the sun so low behind, the eastern shore of the lagoon is not the place to start. Shadows are long and the low open banks show the fisherman in silhouette with his shadow falling across the path of the trout. It is possible to catch fish from this shore with a great deal of care and a long cast but the far bank gives the best chance of a fish.

Once in position the further advantages of looking into the sun are obvious, every whirl and eddy on the surface can be seen clearly, every weedbed breaking the water shows up as black on golden water, and more important the leader can be seen with ease at twenty metres.

I described the fish movement as swirls for that is what they are, not rises as the fish are not feeding on the surface but below it. Even in a metre of water there is disturbance on the surface for these fish are big.

Looking at the water tiny dimples form and disappear, so many that you look up involuntarily to see where the rain is coming from on such a clear morning, but it's not raining. There are few midges in the air so these dimples do not indicate a hatch. Looking into the water close to the edge reveals all. A small creature swims jerkily to the surface, pauses, then swims even more jerkily back to the haven of weed below. Then another makes the trip, and another. The waterboatmen repeat the journey to the surface for air at regular intervals, and the myriads of these insects that live in this fertile lagoon form a constant traffic to and from the surface. Each time one leaves the weed and moves into open water it is exposed to predators, the most prolific being the trout.

Because the waterboatman swims quickly to spend as little time as possible on the trout's dinner table, the trout in turn must act quickly to seize its prey, hence the swirl on the surface. The surface disturbance helps the fisherman locate a feeding fish. But between swirls there is no surface indication of the fish's movement unless the water is shallow in this peaty lagoon. Once a fish has swirled twice, however, the general direction of the fish's movement is established and a suitable imitation can be cast in front of it.

The imitation hits the water with a small splash and begins to sink exactly like the real waterboatman. The leader tippet gradually draws under pulled by the sinking fly. The fish spots the fly, opens its mouth and takes the fly while continuing to swim in the same direction. The leader draws to the side and you strike.

Trout can often be spooked by casting a fly too close to them. This is rarely the case with the Waterboatman. Trout expect the disturbance on the surface and the sudden appearance of the insect. Of course a fish will scare if it sees the leader, or the fly line lands too close so care should be taken to make sure the fly is the part of your tackle closest to the fish.

In my experience it doesn't pay to strike until the leader draws away. The swirl produced by the fish is usually caused when it accelerates towards the fly, so the disturbance occurs fractionally before the take. Strikes to the swirl will often miss the fish.

Stalking fish feeding on waterboatmen can provide some real nerve tingling action, especially if you think the fish feeding in front of you is a big one. Success depends on anticipation and accurate casting. If you size up the fish's movements and get the fly in front of the trout without spooking it there is a good chance of a take. One or two casts are all that should be necessary to do the trick. If there is no take, wait until the fish moves again. Spraying casts all over the water hoping to locate the fish usually results in the fish being scared by the line falling on top of it.

I find when fishing the Waterboatman that I spend a lot more time standing and watching than actually fishing, and this is true for a lot of stillwater fishing. The most successful anglers probably make fewer casts than those that enjoy less success.

In fertile stillwaters waterboatmen and their close relation the backswimmers are present in their millions. I saw so many waterboatmen on one water that I have fished that the bottom could not be seen. As far as the trout were concerned it must have been like waterboatmen soup. Because these insects are present in such numbers, and are an easily accessible food source, the trout in such waters grow big and often are plentiful.

Because of the size of fish regularly caught, and the fact the fish are moving while they take the fly, a strong leader tippet is called for. I usually use a tippet of about 3kg breaking strain, only dropping as low as 2kg if the water is clear and the fish are very wary.

The lagoon that I described in my mind's eye is an oxbow lagoon of the Taieri on the Maniototo plain, but the waterboatman, and to a lesser extent the backswimmer, can be found in many stillwaters. The waterboatmen can be found in good numbers in rivers too, in the slower-moving weedy stretches and backwaters. Even quite small backwaters have their population of waterboatmen. A suitable waterboatman imitation can turn a poor day on a river into an occasion to remember by accounting for a few backwater trout, which are often bigger than average for the stream.

The Mataura is a river that has lots of backwaters throughout its length, and good bags of fish can be had by concentrating on the backwaters alone — if you can drag yourself away from the main river. Waterboatmen abound in Mataura backwaters and the trout regularly feed on them.

Fishing with an Australian friend near Athol on the upper Mataura, we came upon a small backwater with several fallen trees in it. We could see three good fish cruising around, one of them much bigger than the others. I asked Howard if he had any waterboatmen imitations. He hadn't, so I gave him one of mine. There were trees and bushes all round us but Howard put the fly in front of the big fish first cast. The fish accelerated towards the fly and took it on the run and as soon as Howard set the hook the fish headed for the trees. Several times it tried to go under the sunken logs, but each time it was turned at the last minute. Eventually Howard landed the fish, which was over 2.5kg, and we examined the stomach contents which consisted of a large number of water-boatmen and a few snails. As Howard was playing his fish an even larger one emerged from under the trees, at least 3kg we guessed. This fish didn't like the commotion we created and disappeared. A few weeks later I had another look at the backwater but didn't see the big one again, or any others for that matter.

Sometimes if fish are not feeding with any consistency, they can be tempted to take by retrieving the fly in short jerks. The fly is cast in front of a cruising fish and as soon as you think it has been seen, pull in 10-15 centimetres of line at a time with a short pause in between. The fish will think (always supposing fish think) the tasty morsel is escaping and rush over and grab it. At times trout can pick up and eject the fly with amazing speed and a fair percentage of fish will be lost when they have been induced to take. I still remember one large Mataura backwater where I had ten fish take the Waterboatman in half an hour. I hooked six of them but didn't land any. I just couldn't seem to strike fast enough. A couple of them actually took and ejected the fly before I could move the rod, even though I could see everything plainly in the crystal clear water. Luckily the fishing was good on the main river which went some way towards compensating for the disaster on the backwater.

Because fish feeding on waterboatmen are usually cruising over a considerable distance, it is often possible to stand in one place and have the fish come to you rather than the other way round. If there are a lot of fish feeding in one area, a fish should be led away from the others as soon as it is hooked so as not to disturb them. In this way several fish can be caught in quick succession. I have found that such intense feeding on waterboatmen can be limited to one location, and be of short duration, so you have to make the most of such opportunities when they arise.

Whether in river backwaters or lakes, trout will swim into very shallow water to feed, especially in the half light before sunrise or after sunset. When feeding on waterboatmen trout will cruise very slowly if there is just enough water to cover their backs. They only speed up and give themselves away when taking a waterboatman. On other occasions the fish will stay in deeper water most of the time, making short sharp dashes into the shallows to grab their prey. In the light of this behaviour it is sensible to stand and watch for a few minutes before beginning to fish, preferably well back from the water's edge. Then, having located a moving fish, get into position using all available cover that will enable you to cover the fish. As Lord Baden-Powell said, 'time spent in reconnaissance is never wasted' and this is true for all types of fly fishing.

To conclude this chapter, a little story to illustrate the points made in the last paragraph. It was a fine calm morning on Lake Benmore and as I approached the water I could see quite a number of fish moving in the shallows. A long narrow point ran out into the lake and several trout were feeding close in on each side of it. I crept into position about halfway along the point with the water equidistant on either side of me. The first fish moved to the left and it took the waterboatman as soon as it hit the water. I set the hook, the fish took off for deep water, jumped once, and the hook came out. Fish were still moving to my right, so turning through 180 degrees I covered the nearest which obligingly took the fly and was soon on the bank. Without standing up I picked up the fish and removed the fly. Turning back to the left I repeated the trick with another fish. By the time I'd landed that one another was moving to the right and — you've guessed it — it was soon on the bank with the others. So four fish hooked and three landed in about ten minutes while kneeling in one spot.

Like all the flies in this book the waterboatman isn't infallible but at times it's easy to imagine it is.

DEER HAIR SEDGE

Some fly fishers love night fishing, others hate it. I love it. I've had some fantastic fishing in the dark but I've also had some desperate disappointments too. Night fishing is either all go or totally dead. As far as I'm concerned the good times more than make up for those that are less productive. The main attraction of fishing in the dark is the rise to sedges, and when I think of sedge rises three rivers spring to mind, the Waiau, the Clutha and the Waitaki. All are big rivers, all hold a large population of trout, and all hold both brown trout and rainbow with the addition of a few landlocked atlantic salmon in the Waiau.

To keep sedge fishing in perspective I'll tell you about two consecutive evenings on the Clutha between the outlet and Albert-town. It was the middle of February and we were enjoying some fine weather at Wanaka, but the wind had a nasty habit of spoiling things, from the fishing point of view, by springing up in the after-noon. As often as not the wind just kept blowing until well after dark. Not ideal for sedge fishing. But it's hard to miss out on an evening's fishing with the Clutha only ten minutes away, despite the wind.

After looking at and briefly fishing a couple of places which were too exposed to the wind, I found a nice bit of water with some trees providing a little shelter. There were very few sedges about, not a good sign. It was quite dark and the only evidence of feeding fish was the odd splash somewhere in the distance.

I had a size 10 Deer Hair Sedge knotted to my 3kg breaking strain tippet and I cast out in front of me a few metres and allowed the current to carry the fly around towards the bank. When the fly left the main current and slowed as it came into quieter water, I began retrieving line with my left hand, slowly at first, then gradually increasing the speed as the fly came into the slack water right against the bank. The next cast was lengthened a couple of metres and the process repeated. I always start with a short line as fish often feed very close to the bank in the dark and I've caught fish only 2 or 3 metres away even when wading. After half a dozen or so casts I was fishing a comfortable length of line and didn't lengthen any more but moved downstream a step every other cast. This method can be a bit boring, especially when there are no rises to cast to and not much chance of anything at all happening. I'd caught fish on the two previous nights and didn't want to spoil my record, so I was prepared to flog away within reasonable limits until I got a fish. As it turned out I didn't have too long to wait. After about 15 minutes there was a splashy rise and a heavy pull just as the fly started to leave the current and move into slack water. I lifted the rod and felt a solid resistance. The fish took off for the middle of the river, a long way off at this point, jumping as it went. The aerobatics soon tired the fish out and a beautiful short fat rainbow of 1.6kg was soon beached. I packed in while I was ahead and much to everyone's amazement I was home by 11 p.m.

The following day I reconnoitred a stretch of water just down from the outlet that I intended to fish that evening. Very few fish were lying within reach but I could see a lot of fish lying deep. There seemed to be a particular concentration of fish near some large weedbeds and I thought it would be worth a try in the dark.

It was warm and calm when I arrived at the water, perfect. I tackled up and walked down river. There were quite a few sedges in the trees but only a few on the water. However, already a few fish were rising, a good sign. I started fishing down and across with the Deer Hair Sedge, just as I had the previous evening, and soon hooked a nice rainbow. A good start as it was still fairly light. I fished on but didn't touch another fish for quite a while. By then it was quite dark so I decided to head downstream and fish the weedbeds I'd looked at in the morning.

I waded into position at the upstream end of the top weedbed. There was smooth deep water between the weed and the middle of the river and a narrow, shallow channel between the weed and my bank. From my position I could cover both sides of the weed with ease. I had only been fishing a minute or two and a fish rose in the shallow channel, then another, and then one rose on the deep side of the weeds. All were quite a long cast almost straight downstream from me.

I cast the sedge to the spot where the nearest fish had risen and began to slowly retrieve line making the fly skate across the surface. There was a surge in the water where I guessed my fly to be but I didn't feel a take. I fished the cast out and landed the fly in the same area again. This time there was a savage take. I struck and the fish thrashed on the surface and came off. Fish still continued to move and I covered one of them. It took straight away and I walked it upstream away from the others and beached it on a sandbank. By the time I was back in position several more fish were rising well within range. In the next few minutes I hooked and lost two of them. Not a very good percentage landing only one out of four fish hooked. That's the problem with fishing straight downstream. The fish take the fly from behind and are facing the direction in which the strike is made and the fly can pull straight out. Striking at an angle to the direction in which the fish are facing greatly increases the chance of hooking them.

I didn't think there was much sense in standing there losing fish so I moved back upstream. A cool sou'westerly breeze sprang up and rippled the water, a bad sign. I continued to fish but without success until about 11.30 p.m. when the breeze died away and fish started to rise steadily. By the number of sedges that were crawling over my hands or bumping into my face there must have been a lot on the water.

The water along my bank was slow moving and several fish were rising where this slack water met the main current. When a fish rose I waded within range of it but only slightly upstream of the fish. I cast just above and beyond where I guessed the fish to be. It's all guess work in the dark as it is difficult to estimate how far away the fly is landing. One method I use to ensure the area where the fish rise is covered by at least one cast is to purposely cast short on the first cast then fish in the same direction with several more casts but lengthening the line by a metre or so each time. This ploy certainly did the trick that night. I landed three good fish in the next half hour; one of them took really hard and headed for the far side of the river. The tail end of my fly line had long since disappeared through the tip ring before the fish stopped running. It felt very heavy as the whole of my fly line was in the water with the current pressing against it. At times like that it's good to know the leader is 3kg breaking strain.

Eventually I brought the fish to shore and ran it on to the gravel, a beautiful browny of over 2kg. I switched on my torch to remove the fly from the fish and noticed the gravel was crawling with sedges, mostly small dark ones.

I was soon back in action but didn't touch a fish for a while. Strangely enough the rises in front of me were quite sedate affairs, reminiscent of rises to mayflies rather than the splashing, slashing rises to sedges. I don't usually like to shine my torch across the water but my curiosity got the better of me and I did just that. There were a lot of sedges in the air but not so many on the water, and the ones that were on the water were quite large. The size 10 seemed to have lost its attraction so I tied on the same pattern tied on a 10 long shank hook. After a few casts I hooked a fish fairly close in. It took off and I dropped the bunch of line I'd gathered in my hand on the water. The line started to hurtle out through the rod rings as they headed off. All was going well until the rod was almost wrenched out of my hand; then all went slack. A loop of fly line had caught around the butt ring and the leader had broken. Life's like that.

I tied on another sedge of the same size and over the next half hour landed four more fish. By now it was half past midnight and I thought it about time I made my way back to the car in case it had turned into a pumpkin. I'd had enough action for one night anyway; nine good fish, four rainbows and five browns all between 1kg and 2.5kg. Sedge fishing at its best.

I have emphasised good imitation and good presentation when fishing the various imitations in this book — all very logical — but this logic seems to fall apart where these adult sedge imitations are concerned. Any trout that I keep have their stomach contents examined to see if there are any lessons to be learnt. It was immediately apparent that the majority of trout I'd caught on the deer hair sedge had few adult sedges in them. Many had been feeding almost exclusively on sedge pupae on their way to the surface to hatch. Even the trout with the most adult sedges in them would have ten times as many pupae in their stomachs. All this indicates that the pupae are there in greater numbers and are more readily available to the trout. So why do the trout take the odd adult or the floating imitation? I haven't got a sound logical answer to this question but there are a few points that throw some light on the subject.

Trout are always looking for a good return on the energy they expend to catch their food. So if a tasty morsel presents itself on a plate they are not going to refuse it. If an adult sedge drifts close by it presents an opportunity too good to be missed. The key word here is drifts. If the adult sedge rushes past, the trout would need to expend too much energy to capture it. This may also help explain why the skated imitation is taken mainly just as it starts to skate or when it is directly downstream especially in fast water. In slow water the takes are more evenly spread throughout the arc the fly describes on the water, but still the majority of takes are at the beginning and end of the swing.

The logical conclusion from the above observations is that the sedge should be fished as slowly as possible. There are two ways to do this, either fish the imitation dead drift or let the fly hang in the current over the fish's feeding position. Both these ploys work, but dead drift is more effective as fish are more positively hooked. When the fly hangs in the current any pull to set the hook tends to pull the hook out of its mouth. When fishing dead drift the pull is from behind and the hook is pulled further into the fish's mouth.

This dead drift technique, effectively fishing the sedge like a mayfly imitation, really works and the great advantage is very few fish are lost once the hook is set. Earlier in this chapter I mentioned the gentle rises of the trout that made me check what they were rising to by shining my torch on the water, well I'm sure the fish were taking adult sedges that were drifting rather than skittering across the surface.

Since I first tried fishing the sedge dead drift on the Taieri five seasons ago I've tried the technique many times, and often I've skated the sedge over a rising fish without response, then covered it dead drift and caught it. When fishing dead drift in the dark the take is detected by sound and sight usually in that order. Even on quite dark nights it is possible to see the rings of a rise but the sound is usually heard first. Strike immediately you are aware of a take and the fish is as good as yours.

Why, you may well ask, would it not be easier and more effective to fish a sedge pupae imitation if the trout are feeding predominantly on pupae? I think the answer lies in presentation. It is much more difficult to make a pupae imitation act like the real thing than it is to make the adult act like a real sedge, especially in a big river fishing a long line. Fishing a wet sedge down and across to imitate a sedge pupae does work but no better than fishing a dry adult imitation, and certainly far more fish are lost before they are landed. It is possible to catch fish on pupae imitations, especially on small rivers, but that is beyond the scope of this chapter.

When fishing sedge rises on big rivers or small rivers during the day or in the dark I wouldn't be without my Deer Hair Sedges. I carry them in a range of sizes, 14s for daylight and up to 10 long shanks for dark nights.

HARE'S EAR NYMPH

Without doubt the Hare's Ear Nymph (H.E.N.) is a mayfly nymph imitation and a very good one too, but equally without doubt it is also taken by trout for lots of other creatures. I've caught trout on a H.E.N. when they've been feeding on cased caddis larvae, free-swimming caddis larvae, midge pupae, corixae, snails, damsel fly nymphs and willow grub. I'm not saying that it is the universal fish catcher but on occasions that description would seem to fit.

One such occasion was a hot calm cloudless day on the Waipahi in mid-December. I walked downstream for about 3km from where I'd parked the car. Although I kept well back from the water so as not to disturb any fish, I could see the river most of the time and kept an eye open for signs of fish feeding. In the half hour or so it took to walk the distance not a single rise or swirl did I see, much to my disappointment. The river was lowish with just that slight tinge of peatiness that is typical of the Waipahi. I use the H.E.N. as an exploring nymph much as I use the Coch-y-bondhu as an exploring dry fly, so when I reached the ripple I decided to start on I tied on a size 12 H.E.N. The Waipahi has recently gone into a decline but at that time there was a vast amount of underwater food available to trout. There was an abundance of mayfly nymphs and caddis larvae so it seemed logical that, since the fish weren't feeding on the surface, there would be a fair proportion of the trout feeding on these creatures.

The first ripple produced two trout on the H.E.N. One was small and was returned, the other kept and the stomach contents examined. It contained a mixture of mayfly nymphs, sedge pupae, cased caddis and snails. No reason to change flies. Each succeeding ripple produced fish. The sky clouded over in the afternoon but the trout continued to feed and take the H.E.N. By the time I'd fished

Fishing a mayfly rise on the Otamita in the spring. (Photo Murray Smart)

A back country brown, 2.5kg and in superb condition. It fell to a Woolly Caddis. (Photo Mike Weddell)

(Above) *South Island rainbow
don't come much better than
this 2.75kg fish taken from
the Whitestone on a Hare's
Ear Nymph.*
(Photo Mike Weddell)

*Casting a Hare's Ear Nymph
into likely pockets on the
Waiwera.*
(Photo Murray Smart)

Good coch-y-bondhu water on a high country stream.
(Photo John Highton)

(Below) *This fat brown was taken on a Corixa during an outing to Rutherford's Dam in the Maniototo.* (Photo Phil Lind)

Excellent sedge water on the Upper Clutha just below the outlet of Lake Wanaka. (Photo John Highton)

A typical leafy stretch on the Upper Mataura near Garston.
(Photo Mike Weddell)

The popular and picturesque Paddock Bay, Lake Wanaka.
(Photo John Highton)

Perfect conditions to fish the dawn rise on Lake Benmore.
(Photo Bill McLay)

Artificials and Naturals

Coch-y-bondhu

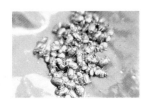

Brown beetle

Green beetle

Black and Peacock

Snails

Woolly Caddis

Sandy Cased Caddis

Artificials and Naturals

No Hackle Dun

Mayfly Dun

Spinner

Spent Spinner

Live Spinner

Corixa

Waterboatmen

Artificials and Naturals

Midge

Midge Pupa

Deer Hair Sedge

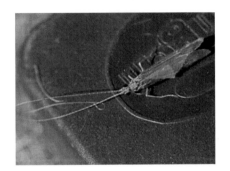

Adult Sedge

Hare's Ear

Pheasant Tail

Mayfly Nymph

back to the car I'd landed twenty-five trout and lost several others. Of the trout I kept the food forms in their stomachs were many and varied — brown beetles, green beetles, adult sedge, sedge pupae, mayfly nymphs, cased caddis larvae and caseless caddis larvae. However that is only part of the story.

When trout are feeding selectively the imitation to be used is more critical. Selective feeding usually means there are large numbers of the particular food form available to the trout, and that this food form is easily distinguishable from other forms by looks or behaviour. Selection by the trout of one particular creature as food does not necessarily mean that the trout deliberately rejects other forms of food. The fact that a trout takes up a particular station in the river may prevent it from being aware of other food forms. For example, if a trout is lying just under the surface taking mayfly nymphs that are about to hatch it will be oblivious to any sandy cased caddis that are being carried along by the current close to the riverbed. In this case the trout is looking up for its prey and it cannot see what is going on below. Then there are occasions when trout become locked on to a particular food form. Several food forms may be available to the fish but only one is selected. Usually the one that is selected is the one that is most plentiful, but sometimes because it involves less energy expenditure.

All of this has many implications of how and where a particular imitation is fished. This is especially true when fishing a mayfly nymph imitation such as the H.E.N. The first thing that has to be taken into account is what the mayfly nymphs themselves are doing. This may be taken as a presumption that the trout are feeding on mayfly nymphs and on some rivers this is a reasonable starting point. For instance on the middle and upper Mataura mayfly nymphs can form up to 70 per cent of the trout's diet.

If there is a hatch of duns in progress there would be nymphs swimming towards the surface making them an easy target for a hungry trout. If there is no hatch most of the nymphs in a particular stretch of river would be on the bottom, either on or underneath stones and fairly inaccessible to trout except for the odd nymph that is washed off its stone by the current. If this was the whole picture opportunities for fishing the mayfly nymph would seem fairly restricted. Luckily it is not the whole picture. Mayfly nymphs migrate downstream at regular intervals. What triggers off the migration is a mystery and the time span from day to day varies considerably. Of course, you can't see the nymph migration unless you have a fine net in the water close to the riverbed and examine it regularly. When the number of nymphs in the net suddenly increases the migration has started.

In fly fishing it doesn't pay to hang around waiting for something obvious to happen. If you did you wouldn't get much fishing done. This is especially true when fishing the nymph. Fish feeding on dislodged or migrating nymphs are not obvious to the fisherman unless they are in shallow water as these nymphs will be close to the bottom. Logically the fisherman's imitation should be close to the bottom too. To ensure the fly gets down deep it is a good idea to incorporate some weight in the dressing by adding lead wire to the hook, especially if the river is deep enough or fast enough to prevent an unweighted model sinking.

My approach is if I'm on the water, and nothing obvious is happening, I fish a weighted size 12 H.E.N. There's a chance of picking up trout that are feeding on anything that comes along, and if and when the nymph migration starts, my imitation is in the right place to take advantage of it. If something else happens in the meantime it's just as easy to change to a more appropriate pattern. All the likely holding and feeding water is fished methodically. It may become a bit monotonous, but you've got to believe there are some fish feeding somewhere, otherwise you might as well go home.

Looking through my fishing diary I read of many instances of picking up the odd fish on the H.E.N., then suddenly taking fish after fish, then equally as suddenly they stopped taking. One instance I can clearly recall (angler's clear recollections are remarkably unreliable so I checked in my diary too) was on the Mataura above Ardlussa bridge a couple of seasons ago. Soon after starting I saw a couple of fish feeding at the tail of a shallow flat. They both took a slightly weighted size 12 H.E.N. without too much trouble. Then things slowed up a bit. There were few fish moving so I fished blind in all the likely places without much joy. By mid-afternoon I'd only picked up another couple of fish on the same fly. Then I came to a long flat that was about 0.5 metre deep at its top end. The light was just right and I could see several fish actively feeding close to the bottom. I cast the same weighted nymph to the nearest fish and it took first time. It turned to one side, turned back again, my leader pulled under and I struck. I towed the fish away downstream to avoid scaring the others. They were still feeding flat out when I moved into position to cover the next fish. Over the next hour I took eight fish from 0.75-1.5kg from that short stretch of water. All were full of mayfly nymphs. Although there had been duns on the water all day, the number of duns didn't increase after all this fish activity, showing that the large number of nymphs moving were not doing so because they were going to hatch. If they had been in the process of hatching I would probably have needed a different approach.

The scene is again the Mataura, this time on the upper reaches near Athol. It was late autumn and the water was cool and as usual at this time of year there wasn't much fish or insect activity until early afternoon. I'd already caught a nice fish on the weighted nymph in the morning but had had little joy since then.

I came to a typical upper Mataura stretch of water. Willows down one side, gravel on the other with a width of about 15 metres of water. There was a good ripple at the head which gradually smoothed out over the next 40 metres. I could see four fish lined up one behind the other where the ripple was almost spent. They were actively feeding, moving from side to side picking up mayfly nymphs I reckoned. This was not pure guesswork as the odd dun had begun to hatch.

The fish at the back of the line was the smallest but I'd have to catch it as I would scare it if I went for the bigger fish first. Everything seemed set for a classic bit of fishing, but fishing isn't usually as simple as that. The little fish wouldn't touch my nymph so I tied on a light size 14 and it took straight away. I pulled it downstream, landed and released it and the others were still feeding quite happily. The next fish took the size 14 without hesitation and I had a struggle to keep it out of the trees on the far side. Eventually I beached it, a nice fish of just over 1.5kg. I was using a tippet of 1.75kg breaking strain because of the clarity of the water and bright sun so I tested it to make sure the fish hadn't weakened it. It seemed sound and I didn't renew it although I usually tie on a new tippet after a sizeable fish has been landed with it.

The next fish didn't like the look of the nymph for some reason that escaped me and slid quietly away under the trees on the far side. The fourth fish took and headed for the trees too, but the tippet broke. Now landing only two out of four fish is nothing to crow about but it does illustrate how the right fly in the right place, that is, high in the water, will be readily accepted by fish, whereas the same fly too deep will be ignored. Just to reinforce this lesson, as the hatch petered out I again caught fish on the heavier nymph yet in similar water to the more selective trout.

I've already said that the H.E.N. is a good general pattern and that fishing it at the correct level in the water is critical. There is, however, one other factor that can be critical at times and that is movement. Usually a nymph imitation should be fished dead drift with no imparted movement other than that given to it by the current. But when the creature the nymph is imitating is an active swimmer this may not be enough. I have caught many trout on H.E.N. that had been feeding on sedge pupae and these insects can swim very quickly when rising to the surface to hatch. Often a conscious effort is needed on the part of the angler to impart this movement to the fly although it can happen by accident. There would be few fly fishers who hadn't hooked a trout just as they were lifting the rod to make a cast. The take comes as the fly is accelerating towards the surface exactly as a sedge pupa does. Being aware of this helps a fly fisher to make deliberate use of this action and can result in fish caught which would otherwise have been missed.

I can remember one occasion when I had the opportunity to observe this in great detail at close range. It was on the upper Ahuriri, the water was clear and the sun was shining. I was walking along a high cut bank and I spotted a fish feeding close against the bank, about 1.5 metres down. I crawled into position behind the fish only about 5 metres away. I could see every spot on its back and the fish looked in good condition. Every now and then it swung to one side or the other and took something although I could not see what. I had a slightly weighted H.E.N. on and worked out a few metres of line well to one side of the fish in case I scared it. I cast well upstream to give the nymph time to get down to the fish's level by the time it reached it. As the nymph went past the trout turned towards the fly but turned away without touching it. I was surprised to say the least. Never mind, it would be taken next time as I was sure the fish was feeding on mayfly nymphs. But the trout totally ignored the H.E.N. on the second and on each of several successive casts. I could not think of a logical reason why it refused.

I thought I'd try something different. I tied on a size 10 Coch-y-bondhu hoping it might be tempting enough to bring the trout to the surface. It didn't. I tied on a Pheasant Tail Nymph but I couldn't think why it would take that when it'd refused the H.E.N. The fish followed my logic this time, besides I didn't think I was getting the fly deep enough.

I stopped fishing and just watched for a while. I noticed a small sedge hatch and flutter away, and a few minutes later I saw another. At the same time I was watching the fish continuing to feed and I realised that not only did the trout turn to the side to take, it also came up in the water and then dropped down deeper again. It had to be taking sedge pupae. I tied on the original weighted H.E.N., cast well above the trout and when I thought the nymph was near the fish I lifted the rod. As the nymph rose in the water the fish came up and took it. It was a beautiful short deep fish of 1.75kg, quite silvery as many of these upper Ahuriri fish are. A post mortem revealed of course that it had been feeding on sedge pupae.

The Hare's Ear Nymph has not been my top fish-catching fly every season but it accounts for more than its share of fish. It is the pattern that I carry in the greatest range of sizes and weights. I use sizes 10-16 and varying in weight from as heavy as possible, while still being able to cast it, to incorporating buoyant materials to keep it near the surface.

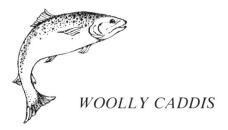

WOOLLY CADDIS

This fly is different to the others in this book as it is designed not to imitate a particular creature, but is a rough imitation of several creatures on which trout feed. Its attractiveness is due, I'm sure, to its weight rather than its shape or colour. Also the great majority of fish I've caught with it have been in back country waters rather than sedate rain fed streams. I find it difficult to state with accuracy exactly when this imitation is most useful. I suppose I use it where there appears to be no predominance of a particular food form, and when I think trout are feeding opportunistically.

Many of the fish I've caught on this pattern have had cased caddis larvae in them and it is not unlike a cased caddis, but many of them have had sedge pupae and larger mayfly nymphs in them too. And I've found stonefly fly nymphs in fish caught on it and it certainly doesn't look like a stonefly nymph.

The main constituent of the fly is lead, lots of lead to make sure it sinks a long way in a short time. Because of the weight of the fly it requires a degree of casting skill to be able to fish it safely. To help the leader straighten the tippet should be heavy, at least 3kg breaking strain.

Despite the vagueness of this introduction to the pattern, a story or two about the fly's use will illustrate its efficiency.

The first instance was on the Omarama stream where a nice fish lay in about a metre of water. The current was quite strong to the fish's left and every so often it turned into the current and picked up a morsel. I tried a Hare's Ear Nymph with a bit of weight in it but the fish didn't respond. I could see that the fly was being whisked away by the current before it got down to the fish's level, so I tied on a heavier Hare's Ear but that didn't work either. I tried casting this fly further upstream to give it time to sink, but because the near part of the fly line was lying on slack water the fly dragged quickly and was pulled back to the surface resulting in it being totally ignored by the fish, always supposing it was aware of it in the first place. I tied on my heaviest size 10 Woolly Caddis, cast it a metre or so above the fish which obligingly turned into the current to take it at the first pass. It wasn't a monster, just over a kilogram but very welcome on a day when fish had been hard to find. This fish had mostly cased caddis in its gut.

The general appeal of this pattern was demonstrated yet again on the Omarama stream. (By the way, small streams are often good research and development waters, as fish can be spotted and watched closely for their reactions to flies.) In larger waters when fishing blind it is impossible to judge fish's reactions, always supposing there were fish there to start with. Even if a good bag is taken fishing blind more fish could have refused the fly than had taken it, and you never know. On small streams I find a large percentage of fish spotted are caught as patterns can be changed if they are refused.

On this occasion on the Omarama stream the fish was lying in deep water close against an overhanging bank. The current swept round a corner a metre above the fish leaving a triangle of slack water for it to lie in. This fish was feeding flat out. It had to be feeding on mayfly nymphs or caddis larvae from its rate of feeding and the depth it was lying at. I had a Hare's Ear Nymph on already and tried it several times, but I knew I wasn't getting down to the fish. I could see its every movement as it was only about 3 metres away from me. I put on a Woolly Caddis size 10 and even with such a heavy fly had difficulty getting it deep enough on the right track to pass close to the fish. There were no refusals I'm sure, it was simply that my initial efforts didn't put the fly in a position to make it a worthwhile proposition for the fish. The first time it passed by in the fish's feeding lane it took with conviction. A beautiful fish close to 2kg and full of, believe it or not, willow grub! This is still the only fish I've caught feeding near the bottom in deep water that has had willow grub in its gut. A quirk of the current must have carried them down there as they usually float on the surface.

Despite what I've just written about fishing blind in larger rivers this is when the Woolly Caddis really comes into its own. This is especially true in fast, deep waters with a population of rainbows. The idea is to get the fly down deep as quickly as you can by casting as far as possible upstream then letting it drift as long as is feasible.

The takes can come at any time but often when the drag free drift ends, the line tightens and the fly just begins to lift in the water. Suddenly everything tightens, you strike and a fish is on, probably securely hooked before you strike due to the tight line and the speed of the fly through the water.

A favourite spot on the Tekapo river was perfect for such fishing. I use the past tense as bulldozers have completely transformed the stretch of water into featureless shallows that no self-respecting fish would inhabit. The water used to be confined by high banks and willows in a deep and narrow channel which it positively raced through. It was often possible to spot fish lying close to the bottom, where presumably the current was slacker, with a couple of metres or more of water above them. The old Woolly Caddis did the trick here casting as far upstream as possible and even walking downstream once the cast had been made to prolong the drift and let the fly sink deeper. Often the take would come straight opposite where I stood as much as 30 metres below where the fly first entered the water. I have taken several fish in quick succession on the Woolly Caddis on this short stretch of water. All the fish I've caught in the Tekapo have had a predominance of mayfly nymphs in their diet although nearly always they had some cased caddis in them too.

In fact the Tekapo has a good population of mayflies and it is rare to visit the river without seeing a hatch of some sort. So if the fish are not actually rising a general nymph will do the trick.

From what I've written so far it would appear that the Woolly Caddis works partly because of its weight, and partly because of the water speed preventing the fish getting a good look at it. A fair assumption but that is not so. I've caught several very good fish in clear still water on this pattern. On one occasion I found a good fish lying in a quiet backwater facing downstream picking up the odd morsel as it drifted past. Luckily the fish didn't spot me which was surprising as I was within 6 metres of it before I saw it. I ducked down out of sight and circled round behind the fish and took up a position where I could easily get the fly to it. I already had a heavy size 10 Woolly Caddis on and perhaps it would have been more sensible to change to a smaller, lighter fly in such calm, clear water. However it didn't make any difference; the fly splatted into the water less than a metre from the fish's nose. It moved straight for the fly and swallowed it. Discovering its mistake the fish took off round the small pool then dashed over the shallows and into the next pool downstream. Eventually I beached it on a gravel bar, a short deep fish of over 3kg.

A few minutes later I was fishing the same fly up a deep section of water next to some overhanging reeds. I couldn't see any fish but it looked a likely spot with good depth and plenty of cover. As the nymph drifted past the reeds I thought I saw a movement deep down. I was contemplating striking when the leader pulled under removing all doubt. I tightened and the fish rushed downstream towards me, went straight past and beached itself on the gravel at the tail of the pool. This trout was over 3kg too and I'd landed, or rather it had landed itself in a few seconds. A fairly respectable brace of fish in a few minutes to the Woolly Caddis.

Because of the types of water I usually fish with this pattern it has produced a greater percentage of 'memorable' fish than any other pattern I use. In fact one particular fly had more than 20 fish of 2kg and over to its credit before it was eventually lost on the bottom of some stream or other. The fly itself is very durable, the hooks used are big and strong, and there is little damage trout teeth can do to the dressing so very few need to be carried, which is just as well considering their weight.

Although I've caught fish in back country waters from the Ahuriri to the Mararoa this isn't the limit of the pattern's usefulness. I've used it on specific occasions on the Mataura and even on small waters like the Waipahi. It is useful in streams where there are short deep pockets of water. A slow sinking fly wouldn't be anywhere near the bottom before it was past the holding water, so a fast sinking fly is needed. There are places on the Mataura where the stream is concentrated into a narrow channel where the water is fast and relatively deep with the only shelter from the current being near the bottom. This is where the trout lie and a deep fly is a must to stand a chance of catching one of them.

I'm sure in smaller sizes this pattern would be just as effective as the Hare's Ear Nymph on many occasions but I'm enough of a believer in having a good imitation of the natural not to try out this theory. But I wouldn't be without a sample of size 10 Woolly Caddis on any back country water.

THE MIDGE PUPA

There's a ditch just down the road from our house and as ditches go it has nothing in particular to recommend it, unless of course, you happen to be a trout fisher. Of course, it hasn't got any trout in it but it does have trout food, lots of trout food. So has the old enamel basin lying in the back garden. Both the ditch and the enamel basin provide an ideal opportunity to study one of the most important food forms for stillwater (and not so stillwater) trout. The creature I'm on about is the chironimid midge, also called the non-biting midge which is just as well, life would be hell if it did bite as there are so many of them around. The adult is often mistaken for a mosquito, which it closely resembles, and although trout do feed on this stage of the insect, it is not so important as far as anglers are concerned.

The larvae of the midge are called bloodworms and any bit of water either in a basin, ditch or lake that stands long enough will have a colony of midge establish itself. The bloodworms, so called because they are wormlike, are red and contain haemoglobin, live in the silt or among dead leaves and algae on the bottom. In suitable conditions bloodworms are there by the million. On occasions the bloodworms protrude from the silt in such vast numbers that the bottom is red with a mass of waving worms. The bloodworm too is taken by trout, but again is not so important to the angler. It is the in between stage of the creature, the pupa that is important to the angler.

The bloodworm pupates, turning into a more insect-like form, the pupa in turn swims to the surface of the water, splits its pupal shuck, and a fully-fledged adult midge steps out and flies off. As a free-swimming creature the pupa exists only a tiny fraction of the time that the bloodworm and adult exist, but for almost the whole of its existence it is readily available to the trout and usually in vast numbers. On a fertile lake literally hundreds of tons of midge would hatch in a year and many tons of trout start out as midge pupae.

Midge pupae are unmistakable; they have characteristic white breathing filaments at the head end, a well-developed thorax with wing cases, and a long curved segmented body. The pupae swim to the surface in greatest numbers in times of poor light, on dull days but predominantly at dawn and dusk. Luckily from the angler's point of view, these creatures are easy to imitate both in looks and action, their only drawback being the large numbers present competing with your imitation for the attention of the trout.

Midge and their pupae vary enormously in size. Relating them to hook sizes they would run from size 20 (maybe even smaller) to size 10. The most common sizes, and of most interest to fly fishers, are 14 and 12. They can vary in colour too: some are red, others green and commonest of all black. Maybe black isn't an adequate description, rather alternate grey and black bands being a better guide for tying an imitation.

Evidence of hatches of midge is seen in the form of columns of adult midge hovering in the lee of trees and bushes. These columns of midge can extend beyond your range of vision with many thousands of adults in each column, and in calm conditions there are many columns and the combined noise of these millions of beating wings fills the air with a soft buzzing sound. On the reservoirs of the English Midlands, where there are enormous hatches of midge, the insects are commonly known as buzzers.

In warm conditions midge hatch very quickly. The pupa arrives at the surface and as it breaks through into the air the skin splits, the adult emerges and flies off almost instantaneously creating a circular ripple on the water as it takes off. When a hatch is in full swing the surface of the water is covered in rings making it look as though it is raining. Among the myriads of rings formed by the emerging adults will be much larger rings, those created by rising trout.

In days when the surface tension of the water is high midge pupae have difficulty in penetrating the surface and spend some time immediately below the surface. If there is a large hatch and there are vast numbers of pupae trying to pierce the surface film, the underside of the water surface must look like a heavily-laden dining table to the trout. At such a time the trout cruise along on the surface taking pupae without effort. The rises are slow and gentle with little disturbance to the water surface. When the hatch is more sparse and the surface tension is low, or there is a ripple on the surface, the pupae swim rapidly towards the surface, hatch instantly, and fly away. On such occasions the trout need to move quickly. The rises are more rapid and there is considerable upheaval of the surface water. When a hatch starts there are spasmodic rises but within a short time midge are hatching in vast numbers and most trout in the vicinity will be feeding on the pupae.

Although as suggested earlier the midge is considered primarily to be of value to the stillwater angler, it is not unusual to find trout feeding on them in the slower sections and backwaters of rivers and streams. I have experienced significant hatches on the Shag, Waipahi and Waimea rivers and on Mataura backwaters. In such places the imitation pupa would be fished as any other nymph fished dead drift in streams, or cast to individual fish in the backwaters.

On stillwaters where there are regular hatches of midge I like to be on the water as dawn is breaking. Unless it is quite warm there is usually little midge activity until it starts to get light. In warm conditions midge will hatch in the hours of darkness too. As the sky lightens the hatch increases and in favourable conditions may last for two or three hours, then often ceases quite suddenly. The reverse happens in the evenings. The light begins to fade and the hatch gains momentum, and from sunset till dark reaches its peak before gradually dying off.

Because midge are present in vast numbers it is common to have a few pupae making the journey to the surface at any time of day. Consequently trout will quite readily pick up a pupa imitation even though there is no general hatch in progress, unless they are totally preoccupied with some other food form.

A rise to a hatch of midge can provide fast action for anglers provided they don't lose their heads with so many rises around them. Tactics in such a position are fairly simple. An imitation of size 14 should be fished with a slow retrieve. Since the concept of speed of retrieve varies considerably from angler to angler I would define slow as about 10cm per second. If there are a lot of fish rising within casting range it is probably better to cast out in the general area of the rises and retrieve the fly, repeating the operation until a fish is hooked. I realise this is easier said than done, there being a great temptation to cast immediately to each rise as it occurs. This is counter-productive for when your fly reaches the position of the rise the fish has moved on and you are always casting behind the fish and it won't see the fly.

If you are close to fish it is sometimes possible to see in which direction they are moving. If they rise regularly and you keep your eye on a particular fish, you can predict where the next rise will be and have your fly there ready and waiting. If the wind is blowing and the water rippled, generally fish will swim directly upwind when feeding so if you see a rise cast upwind a couple of metres and retrieve slowly. The fish will often spot the fly as it hits the water and commencing the retrieve seems to trigger off the fish's desire to grab the fly. If the fish hasn't spotted the fly hit the water the movement of the retrieve will be enough to attract its attention as it gets closer.

Things are so much easier if you can actually see the fish in the water. Often careful positioning in relation to the sun and dark reflection on the water will help. For instance, if there are bushes in the water, looking towards the bushes' reflection enables you to see into the water more easily as it helps eliminate surface glare. Of course, you need to wear polarising glasses as well as getting into the right position.

Once you have located a fish the ploy is the same as casting to rises except the fly can be placed more precisely a metre in front of it. You can then watch the fish's reaction, twitching the fly as the trout gets closer, or if this has scared a few fish just let it sink and that will often do the trick. A rough guide as to how close to a fish you can land a fly is; in open water with little cover, cast further away from the fish as they are generally jumpier if there is no cover close at hand. Conversely, if there is plenty of cover, for instance if the fish is cruising through thick weedbeds or between rushes, the fly can be dropped very close to the fish.

Having got the fly in position the next problem is to detect the take. If the fish is visible, watch for the white of the mouth as it opens and as soon as you see it, tighten by lifting the rod firmly. This applies to all nymph fishing whether on stillwaters or rivers. If the fish cannot be seen well enough watch the leader where it is lying on the surface. As the fly sinks it gradually drags down the floating part of the leader. Any quickening of this rate of sinking should be treated as a take and acted on accordingly. Most times there will be no doubt as the leader will be totally dragged under with a great pull. The problem arises when the fish is moving towards you and takes very gently. The slightest suggestion of a take should be acted upon. In fact, many times I have seen no sign of a take, but just tightened on the off chance a fish had taken to find it firmly attached to the fly.

Ideally the fly should be the part of the tackle that is nearest the fish. This is most easily achieved by being positioned at ninety degrees to the fish's direction of movement. The take is also more easily detected as the end of the leader is dragged sideways as the fish carries on along its chosen path after taking the fly, but this is the ideal and more often than not conditions are far from ideal. We have just got to make the most of them.

Coincidently I have just returned from a three-day trip to Lake Benmore where I fished to trout rising to midge pupae each morning. The water was clear and the water calm and while the light was poor the fish readily accepted a size 14 black midge pupa, but as the sun climbed higher they became harder to deceive. To continue taking fish I reduced the size of the imitation to 16 and fished a fine tippet of 1.8kg breaking strain. The fishing was magnificent, fish rising all around on one occasion and good fish too. One that I hooked a couple of metres from the shore took me on to the backing on its first run for the middle of the lake. It was over 2kg and in great condition.

It is worth emphasising that even good-sized fish come very close inshore if undisturbed. Several of the fish I caught on the trip were cast to from a kneeling position a few metres back from the water's edge. I find that wading just pushes the fish further out or even puts them down altogether. If wading is necessary, do it slowly and get into a position and wait. Use available cover, bushes or reeds or a higher background, either a bank or trees. Remember cover behind you is often just as effective as cover in front, the most important thing is not to be visible against the sky. Once you're in position it doesn't take the fish long to come back within range.

Fishing the midge pupa can be exciting and productive, can also be very exacting. But persevere, it is worth it. Just make sure you have a few midge pupa imitations in your fly box next time you fish a lake.

NO HACKLE DUN

All the classic books of fly fishing heap praise on fishing for fish that are rising to mayflies. Halford and Skues and many others went into literary raptures when relating the practice and theory of dry fly fishing. But early in my career I did little dry fly fishing and tended to dismiss such fishing as being something that was done on chalk streams and rarely anywhere else. Where I learned to fish, anglers were wet fly fishers full stop. When fish rose to large dark olives, blue winged olives or March Browns we tried to ignore the fish and flogged away with wet flies. The excitement of the rise quickly turned to frustration as only a few tiddlers would take our offerings. We were glad when the rise ended and we could start catching fish again.

As I read more about fly fishing, and mixed with fly fishers from other areas, my horizons were widened. First of all I began to use nymphs in addition to our traditional wet flies, then I took the radical step of fishing the dry. The results were not surprising. Not only did I catch fish before and after, but during the rise as well. Not just catching fish during the rise but catching more in its short duration than the wet was producing over a longer period.

Of course it wasn't all plain sailing. Sometimes fish refused my dry fly, most inconsiderate of them I thought at the time. But it was me that was being inconsiderate. I wasn't taking into consideration that the trout decided what was acceptable and not the angler. I began to go through the throes of trying to find the infallible pattern, a pattern to cover all the mayfly rises I would come across in a season. I suppose every fly fisher goes through this phase and on reflection the whole of fly fishing history has been preoccupied with this problem.

I achieved a certain level of success, but as I often caught more fish as the light started to fade in the evening, I realised that my pattern wasn't standing up to the scrutiny of trout in the full light of day. A stroke of luck just at the right time maintained the momentum of my improving ability to catch fish rising to mayflies. It was in the form of a visit by a Dutch friend who is a very good fly tyer, and also very generous to his friend with the flies he tied. He gave me several mayfly dun imitations that didn't use hackles to float them. They had deer hair wings and a wide forked tail to keep them upright. They didn't look much like duns to me, but then again neither did the traditional feather duster duns I'd been using. The flies he gave me were in several sizes from 14 to 22! Yes 22. I did catch one or two fish on 22s but being a bit brisk on the strike I usually just straightened the hook, so 18s were the smallest I regularly fished. I could now catch fish consistently in the full light of day too.

The trout I was fishing for at this time were good subjects on which to try out fly patterns as the water was heavily fished and those fish probably saw more flies in a week than I had in my whole collection. If these flies worked then they had to be good. My friend also gave me some flies that had the wings made from duck primary feathers, but these were, at size 12, rather big to imitate the mayflies that hatched on my river so I didn't try them.

My story now jumps forward a couple of years and moves 20,000 kilometres to New Zealand. In December 1981 I was staying on the banks of the Mataura between Mataura and Wyndham. At this time the river was falling and clearing, still about a third of a metre or so above summer level. Each evening there was a hatch of duns from sunset until dark. The intensity of the hatch depended on the wind. On calm nights the fish rose freely to hatching duns for over an hour. The second night was just such a night.

A few duns started to hatch before sunset but nothing rose so I fished a nymph in a deep ripple and caught a fish. The number of duns increased as the light faded and fish began rising in the ripple. It was a difficult ripple to fish as the water swirled and boiled as it came over rocky reefs. The fish seemed to hang in the current and let it wash them back and forward. A fish would rise in one position and its next rise would be some distance away in no particular direction. Some persistent casting with my Deer Hair Wing Dun produced two nice fish.

Then fish began rising in the slower water above the ripple so I moved in behind them and covered them. They were equally keen to sample my fly and I had another five fish on the bank by the time the rise petered out. I kept only the best fish which was just over 2kg. This was great fishing and it was the same each evening of the trip.

But of course that was no test of the fly as most reasonable imitations work at twilight time. The acid test for the fly, however, did come on that trip. There was a big swirling back eddy off the main river with a better than average trout cruising around it. The fish rose occasionally so I crept into position and waited until it came within casting range. I dropped the fly about half a metre in front of the fish which cruised over and slowly circled round it. Then with nerve wracking slowness it moved towards the fly, rose to the surface and in slow motion sucked the fly in. As it turned down I set the hook and the fish began thrashing on the surface and the hook came out. Although the outcome wasn't entirely successful at least the fly worked in bright sunlight and clear water.

After enjoying considerable success with the Deer Hair Wing Compara Dun I thought I'd try the Mallard Quill Wing pattern. This style looked more like the real dun, to me at least. I tied some up in 16s and 14s to give them a trial.

The first opportunity to use the pattern came during my second visit to the Waipahi in October 1983. It was a cool overcast day that threatened rain and there was a tricky downstream wind blowing. I found several fish rising soon after I started and I covered them with a size 14 No Hackle Dun. I caught three of them but with a bit of a struggle. Part of the reason was the fly dragging as they were lying at the tails of two pools. The line was lying in faster water than the fly and any slack thrown into the leader was soon taken up and the fly dragged after very short drift.

I wandered upstream and fished a nymph in a few ripples as there was no sign of a rise. I was wading up a shallow ripple and casting ahead when my feet went out from under me and I fell in. Dragging myself to my feet and feeling rather undignified I climbed up the bank and thought this seemed a suitable juncture to call it a day and head home. I was emptying out my waders and wringing the water from my shirt and trousers when I noticed a rise a few yards above me. I was dressed in a flash, and despite the rain that had begun falling, and feeling quite cold, I tied on a size 16 No Hackle Dun. Fishing a very short line I covered the fish. It took without hesitation and so did the next one. The wind-ruffled surface and the by now very poor light allowed me to approach very close to the rising fish. This enabled me to attain a drag-free drift especially in the pool tails.

I soon forgot about the cold as I found more fish rising. I have an entry in my fishing diary for that day stating that I caught virtually every fish covered from then on and landed nine in the next two hours.

Since that day I have rarely used the deer hair winged variety and have stuck with the mallard quill. The fly has one disadvantage, it is quite hard to float especially in broken water but is well worth the effort. Both styles are fairly durable and I've had more than half a dozen fish on one fly on several occasions, which isn't bad for any dry fly.

I now use only sizes 14 and 16 of this pattern and it has proved its worth many times. Once when fishing the Mataura near Mandeville I came to a long shallow ripple and could see quite plainly a number of fish very close to the edge just above me. All the fish were feeding flat out, moving from side to side, picking up what I guessed were nymphs. I tried a lightly dressed Hare's Ear Nymph over the first fish and it took easily enough. I led it away downstream to avoid scaring the others and beached the fish on the gravel. I moved back into action covering the next fish without response. It didn't seem a logical move as there were no duns on the water at the time, but I tied on a size 16 No Hackle Dun. The fish took first time, and so did the next three in a row before the fish went off the feed. I examined the gut contents of one of the fish out of curiosity. It was full of emerging duns.

On another occasion on the Waipahi I spotted a good fish holding station towards the tail of a long pool where it rose several times as I got into position to cover it. The No Hackle Dun was a bit bedraggled as I'd already caught several fish on it, but I cast it at the fish anyway. It sank as soon as it landed under a metre above the fish. Lifting the fly straight off again would most likely have scared the fish so I decided to let it drift past before recasting. While I was waiting for the fly to pass the fish I saw it swing to the right and open its mouth. I tightened just in case and sure enough I was securely attached to a nice fish of 1.5kg. Since then I've caught several fish on a sunken No Hackle Dun. This is really upstream wet fly fishing so the No Hackle Dun is quite versatile being both a wet or dry fly on demand.

PHEASANT TAIL NYMPH

From the time I first started fishing I've been an avid reader of fishing books. Some were about salmon fishing and others about fishing in general, but the vast majority were devoted to trout fly fishing. Some of them I didn't think much of, most I enjoyed and one or two I thought were outstanding. One of the latter is a book called *Nymph Fishing in Practice* by Oliver Kite. Both the style and the content appealed to me. The book was informative, easy to read and for me inspirational.

At the time I read it I had only fished wet fly on two rivers and had had only one outing on a lake, so my experience was limited to say the least.

What struck me most about this book was that Kite made catching trout a simple exercise in logic, whereas most other works created an air of mystique and complexity about fly fishing. Kite caught a large percentage of his fish on the Sawyer Pheasant Tail nymph and although he fished mainly in the chalk streams of Hampshire and Wiltshire, I knew enough to realise that this pattern would be a good imitation of the nymphs of the large dark olive that abounded in my home waters. I tied up several according to Kite's instructions and enjoyed considerable success with them.

Subsequently I read Sawyer's *Nymphs and the Trout* in which he tells of the development of the Pheasant Tail Nymph and his technique for fishing it. Sawyer relates how he used the P.T.N. in various countries to good effect. Logically enough on my first trip to New Zealand in 1975 I had a good stock of P.T.N.s with me.

The first trout that fell to the P.T.N. on that trip was a fish of almost 2kg on the Greenstone river and quite a few others fell to the nymph on my trip in to that river. Catching rainbows on the Greenstone is hardly a true test of a fly as they would probably take anything that came their way. One experience of the unsophisticated nature of Greenstone trout springs to mind. I saw a rise by an over-hanging tussock and as I had a Coch-y-bondhu on the end of my leader, that's what I cast to it. It rose nicely enough but I was a little quick on the strike and the fish thrashed on the top and threw the hook. The fish just lay there collecting its thoughts while I, being the supreme optimist, covered it again with the 'Cochy'. Not surprisingly the fish totally ignored it. After two or three goes I decided to try the P.T.N. to see if that was acceptable. It was, and I'd soon landed and returned a wiser if somewhat shaken rainbow.

The P.T.N. was originally devised to imitate the olive nymphs which are free swimmers, the so-called agile darters. The only nymphs in New Zealand that move as freely as the agile darters are *Nesameletus* and *Oniscigater* which are much larger nymphs. Because of its method of construction I don't think the P.T.N. makes a convincing imitation in anything bigger than size 14, and now I only use it in sizes 16 and 14. I know P.T.N.s of sizes 12 and 10 will catch fish but I'm sure when trout are being selective the small sizes are best.

The trout of the Brightwater, a small gin-clear spring-fed tributary of the upper Mataura, are difficult to catch for two reasons. Firstly they are very difficult to approach because of the clarity of the water and, secondly, because they know what a nymph should look like. An Australian friend, Peter Wilson, and I managed to sneak into a suitable fishing position behind what looked like quite a small Brightwater trout by normal standards. Pete had on a dry 'Cochy' and I had on a nymph so Pete was given first shot. The fish ignored his size 12 imitation so my size 14 P.T.N. was next in the queue. The fish moved to it but didn't take it and ignored it on subsequent passes. Pete's turn again this time with a size 14 'Cochy'. Total rejection. I tried a size 16 P.T.N. next and it was taken first time. The fish was over 1.5kg, much bigger than it looked in the water.

Because I use the Hare's Ear as my main nymph pattern, now I reserve the P.T.N. for specific conditions. These are very clear waters and when a very small imitation is called for. The P.T.N. has the added advantage that it sinks smoothly, it doesn't stick in the surface film as nymphs with a dubbed fur body tend to. It is an ideal general pattern for fishing to cruising fish in clear water. It can be plopped in well ahead of the fish which often dash over and grab it as it slowly sinks. I have had a trout travel 5 metres to take a size 16 P.T.N.

The original method of fishing a P.T.N. as devised by Sawyer, was to employ the induced take on fish that were feeding on nymphs swimming towards the surface to hatch. The copper wire gets the nymph below the level of the fish and as the nymph draws near to the trout, the rod is lifted to draw the nymph back to the surface, just as the real nymphs are doing. The theory is that this invokes a reflex action from the fish which grabs the nymph before it gets past.

I've used this method to good effect on the Mataura. One day between Mataura and Wyndham I'd just tackled up and was looking along a high bank for feeding trout, when I spotted two close together. I got into position to cast which was actually just upstream of the fish. I cast the P.T.N. above the top fish and it seemed to ignore it, so I gently lifted the rod and as the nymph lifted past the trout's nose it grabbed the fly. I quickly led the trout away and landed it. Returning I found the other fish still feeding so I repeated the operation. A good start to the day, two casts, two fish.

The first time I fished the Shag river was in November 1980. I remember the day had an inauspicious start when I hooked a good fish on the P.T.N., but the trout soon broke the attachment by charging through a submerged pile of weed and branches. Things soon looked up however when I spotted two good fish that were feeding actively in a ripple. The larger of the two was my target and it took the P.T.N. after a few attempts. At just over 2.5kg it more than made up for the previous loss. Strangely enough the fish had been feeding on bloodworms and there wasn't a sign of mayfly nymphs in its gut.

I caught four more trout that day and they were more conformist than the first trout. All took the P.T.N. and all were taking mayfly nymphs just under the surface. The five fish averaged about 1.8kg.

Of all the flies that I currently carry the P.T.N. is the one I've used the longest and somehow it wouldn't seem quite right to be without it. I even carry a separate box, an old metal hook box, to keep them in, just like Oliver Kite.

THE SPINNER

When a mayfly dun hatches, providing it doesn't fall prey to trout or insect feeding birds, it leaves the water and finds cover in riverside vegetation. At some time over the next 24 hours or so it splits its skin and the mature adult emerges; this is the fly fisher's spinner. It is exactly the same shape as the dun that it emerged from, but there are some basic differences. The wings are transparent and glisten like cellophane, as opposed to the dull opaque wings of the dun. The body colour too is different; spinners of most species have brown bodies and the brown darkens as time passes. The spinners of *Deleatidium* species are a rich mahogany brown by the time they return to the water.

After the spinner emerges from the dun it returns to the water if it is a female. If it is a male it hovers in columns along the river bank, together with thousands of its contemporaries, waiting for a returning female to pass by. When she does the nearest male mates with her, and she continues on her way to the water and deposits her eggs to begin the next generation. One of the consequences of this method of reproduction is that virtually all the spinners on the water are females.

When the female has completed her egg-laying she begins to wilt and if still flying falls to the water. Her wings begin to drop until they are flat on the surface one either side of the body. This is the spent spinner.

Once female spinners return to the water they are exposed to predation by trout until the current dissipates the spent remains. The implication is that the spinner is important from the fly fisher's point of view in creating opportunities to cast to, if not actually catch, rising trout. Some would say the spinners provide the cream of trout fly fishing. But like most good things it takes a little effort to master rises to spinners.

My first success with fish rising to spinners was before I knew what a spinner was. This was on my home river the Coquet which I discovered, many years later, is quite famous for its fall of sherry spinners, the spinner of the blue-winged Olive. G. E. M. Skues mentions in one of his books taking 40 fish with a sherry spinner imitation in one evening on the Coquet.

One particular summer I began dry fly fishing on the Coquet, a fairly radical move as Northumberland is one of the bastions of the wet fly fisher. I had some success and flushed with enthusiasm I fished regularly in the evenings. In fact that August I fished 28 evenings and each evening there was a hatch of B.W.O.s. The hatch usually started just after sunset and continued through the twilight and petered out as the sky darkened about an hour after sunset. Fishing for the trout rising to duns wasn't particularly difficult and even in the sparsest hatches I caught a few fish. Often I would find myself about 3 kilometres downstream of the village by the time the rise ceased.

Walking upstream towards the village the glow of the street lights was reflected from the surface of the water, and it was possible to spot rises even though the after-glow in the western sky had long since disappeared. These rises were very small, just dimples on the surface. At first glance it would seem they were made by undersized fish. One evening I was in no hurry to get home and I waded within range of these dimpling fish, making sure I kept them between me and the village lights. The light wasn't good enough to see my fly, let alone whether it was floating or not. I cast in the general area of the rises and if a rise occurred in the right area I struck. There were a lot of false alarms but enough fish were hooked to keep it interesting. Many nights I caught more fish like this than on the rise to duns at twilight.

Eager to see what the fish were feeding on I examined the gut contents and found what looked like winged pheasant tail nymphs. Some fish had many hundreds in their gut, so whatever it was there were a lot of them around. The colour of the body was exactly the colour of a reddish cock pheasant tail feather. Although I still continued to catch them on a black-bodied fly with a sparse hackle, colour is not so important at night. Strangely enough I don't actually remember seeing a live sherry spinner in the light of day.

I now know that the rises I saw were to spent spinners and by chance my bedraggled hackled dun imitation wouldn't have floated too well and this was a reasonable imitation of a spent spinner given the poor light conditions.

By the time I came to New Zealand I was fairly familiar with the concept of spinners but had still not actually fished to a spinner rise in daylight. I can clearly remember, with the aid of my fishing diary for the '81-'82 season, that I hooked my first fish that was rising to spinners on the Waipahi on 31 October. It was Waipahi Gold Medal day and I'd drawn section 10. I was to fish the upper half of the water in the morning. I started at the tail of a long flat and as I tackled up a good fish rose two or three times, obviously to spent spinners. I had only one spinner imitation in my fly box, a size 14 spent imitation. I tied it on and covered the fish which obligingly took and I hooked it. The fish rushed up the pool and jumped clear of the water and the line went slack. Somewhat disappointed I reeled in to discover the hook had broken. But the lesson was well learned. I tied up some spinner imitations in case they were needed again. Two years later in the Gold Medal I took only three fish and all three were on the spent spinner shortly after starting. But three fish landed and one lost hardly qualifies my spinner imitations to a full chapter, that was only the start.

Those of you that keep a fishing diary, or have an exceptionally good memory, will remember that April of 1982 was a glorious month. Many days were warm, calm and cloudless. I spent the first couple of weekends on the upper Waitaki, but concentrated on the Mataura during the latter half of the month, with the spinner being prominent on the three days that I fished there.

The pattern of events was the same for the first two days, firstly fish moved to nymphs in the ripples and from about midday a hatch of duns started that continued for some time. Then towards evening there was a fall of spinners. Fish rose through till 5.30 p.m. which is when I left. I spent the whole day on two ripples and the intervening pool and landed 17 fish and lost several. And believe it or not, I have a note in my diary that they were difficult to catch. There were so many fish moving I must have cast to a hundred or more, thus explaining the 'difficult to catch' comment.

Spinners drift down the current depositing their eggs and as they die they are washed downstream. Like most objects that float down a river they end up in the slow water along the edges or in back eddies where they lie until eaten by trout or birds. Trout expend as little energy as possible when feeding and a backwater sprinkled with spinners provides a leisurely meal even for the most indolent trout. This is what happened that day on the Mataura. As the sun dropped towards the western horizon spent spinners carpeted the slow moving shallow water adjacent to the gravel beach from which I was fishing. Fish of a kilo and more were cruising with their dorsal fins out of the water sipping down spent spinners at their leisure. I managed to hook and land only three and lost a few others. Fish that cruise in slow shallow water are hard to catch because you need to anticipate where they will be when your fly hits the water. They can easily change direction between their last rise and your fly hitting the water. Generally in shallow water you need to get a dry fly fairly close to a fish to attract it to take, and this is especially so when there are literally dozens of naturals from which to choose its next mouthful.

In the light of subsequent experience I put down my relative lack of success in deceiving spinner-feeding trout that day to the fact that the pattern I was using was at fault.

At this stage I must point out that a fall of spinners is not a phenomenon that you come across every day. In fact I've only fished one rise to spinners on my last four visits to the Mataura, yet the previous five visits all produced a rise to spinners. Even if good spinner rises are infrequent the quality of fishing they produce makes it worthwhile being prepared for them.

I've already mentioned in chapter one how important size is, especially when fishing a spinner imitation. I have found on several occasions that changing to a smaller size often produced the desired result, especially when fishing the spinner on flat water such as at the tails of pools.

Two patterns are needed for spinner fishing and of the two that I have evolved to date, one represents the live spinner and the other the spent spinner. The live imitation has been described above, pheasant tail body, grizzle hackle and tail. The spent imitation has a similar body and tail but two grizzle hackle tips are used for wings and there is no hackle.

To complete the spinner saga I will mention more recent experiences on the Mataura. The first instance took place above Ardlussa bridge in February 1986. It was a warm, calm sunny morning when Dougal Rillstone and I got on to the water at 8.30 a.m. Already fish were moving to spinners. I fished from a position where I could plainly see three nice fish rising to spinners. Even though I was close to the fish and could see them in between rises, it was difficult to cover them as they ranged over such a wide area in the slow, flat water at the tail of a long pool. There wasn't a huge fall of spinners and the fish would move two metres or more to take an individual fly. If fish are holding station in the current a sparse hatch is ideal from the angler's point of view as they take every one that passes including an artificial. In slow water it is a matter of persistent casting until fish and fly meet.

Difficulties encountered in slow water are compounded when the fish are not visible between rises. Again persistence pays off. That morning I caught two of the three fish I could see but it took me almost half an hour.

Before relating another Mataura tale there are several other points that contribute to the success of fishing the spinner. First of all, it is a waste of time fishing a spinner imitation if there are no fish rising, even if there are spinners on the water. Fish will rise to spinners if there are enough to make it worth their while. If there is some other form of food that is more readily available they will choose that every time. The predominance of one particular food form can change quickly. I've fished the Mataura when trout have been feeding on nymphs, duns and spinners all within the hour. Occasionally you will find some fish feeding on spinners, some on nymphs, all at the same time. You need to be alert for such changes, locate a fish and if you aren't sure what it is taking watch individual flies as they drift over the fish and see which are taken. It is a little easier to decide if trout are taking spent spinners as the rises are mere dimples, often deceptively small for the size of the fish making them.

It is important to have on the correct spinner imitation, either spent or otherwise, as the occasion demands. I find fish can often be caught on the spent pattern when they are rising to the live spinner, but rarely the other way round, especially in slow water. The reason is simple, as the fall intensifies there will be spinners on the water that are spent having deposited their eggs early in the fall. Towards the end of the fall most of the spinners will be spent and drifting into slow water and the trout move in after them.

It was mid-April on the Mataura, another glorious day, and John Dean, Dougal Rillstone and I had had some success with the nymph during the day. Dougal had even come across localised hatch of duns and caught a few fish.

We all met up just before sunset at the tail of a long flat when spinners began returning by the thousand, or even the million with their wings reflecting the gold of the setting sun. The previously unrippled flat was boiling with fish feeding on them. I caught a couple on the spinner imitation but soon the shallow margins were coated with the spent insect. I put on a spent pattern and caught two or three more but had to cover a lot of rises to get a take. The fish were rising every few centimetres as they cruised slowly along the gravel beach. My fly had a lot of opposition from the naturals so to make it stand out from the crowd I tied on a size 14, which was bigger than the naturals, and caught four more quite quickly before the rise stopped abruptly. I'd caught eight fish all day and doubled that in only an hour fishing the spinner fall.

To conclude my ravings about spinner fishing, a less spectacular story as far as numbers of fish are concerned, but probably more important as huge spinner falls are the exception rather than the rule.

The scene was again above Ardlussa bridge, this time with Murray Smart and John Dean. The weather was warm and overcast with little wind. Murray and I caught several quite quickly on the tail end of the morning spinner fall. Then it was all hard work. I picked up a good fish on the nymph. Then we saw little action after that. Late in the afternoon there was a sprinkling of spinners on the water but no general rise. I just walked slowly upstream watching carefully for any sign of a rise. I spotted the tiniest of dimples in fairly shallow water close to my bank. I waited but it didn't rise again. I eventually cast a size 16 spinner to the spot and it disappeared in another tiny dimple. The fish was about 1kg. Later I repeated the process in another spot and landed a slightly smaller fish. When walking back downstream to the car in the late afternoon I saw a tiny dimple in shallow water alongside an overhanging grassy bank. Sneaking forward I peered into the water but couldn't see the fish. However I waded into the water a few metres below and cast the spinner close to the bank, another dimple and I tightened into the best fish of the day, 1.5kg.

Spinner fishing isn't easy but is well worth the effort.

TYING THE FLIES

This chapter is a guide to tying the flies covered in this book. It is not meant as an instructional work on fly tying, although anyone familiar with the basics of fly tying should cope with most of the patterns. Several of the patterns described are my own idea of what imitations of certain creatures should look like. You may have better ideas and develop better patterns. I'm sure I'll change a few of them myself over the next few years.

If you asked half a dozen fly tyers to tie a particular pattern the examples they produced would all differ from the others as each have their own ideas of what constitutes a good fly. My own preference is for sparsely tied flies, the logic behind this being that most of the creatures to be imitated are delicate in construction and so the imitation should be delicate too.

Black and Peacock Spider, sizes 16-10

Body: Bronze peacock herl

Hackle: Black hen

I like to tie the body big and round and the hackle sparsely and not too long. To make the body durable I twist the half dozen or so strands of herl around the tying silk before building up the body. A criss-cross pattern builds up the body better than parallel turns which tend to slip over each other.

Coch-y-bondhu, sizes 14-8

Tail: Ginger hackle fibres

Body: Bronze peacock herl or green peacock sword herl

Hackle: Furnace or mixture of black and red hackles

The traditional Coch-y-bondhu doesn't have a tail but has a tag of gold tinsel. I prefer a tail as it aids flotation especially in fast broken water. The body is built up in the same way as for the Black and Peacock Spider. I usually use a minimum of three hackles but usually four either true furnace hackles or alternate red and black hackles. Good furnace hackles are hard to come by.

Corixa, sizes 16-14

Body: Olive green synthetic dubbing material or grey ostrich herl

Legs: Biots from Mallard primary feathers

Back: Dark grey or brown primary feather, hen pheasant, goose, pale turkey, etc.

The naturals vary considerably in colour according to their environment so colour isn't too critical. I tie in the biots as I'm running the silk down to the bend of the hook. Biots by the way are the short very stiff fibres on one side of the quill of a flight feather, in this case those of a mallard. I tie them in together pointing upwards then tie in the feather to form the back, then dub the body. The biots are then parted and the back feather taken between them to keep them apart.

Deer Hair Sedge, sizes 14-10 long shank

Body and Wing: Deer hair

Hackle: If used of a reddish hue

Deer hair is spun on to the hook for almost its full length with a little space being left at the front to wind a hackle. The hair is then clipped to shape and the hackle added last. I think it is important to make sure all the hair is cut away from the inside of the bend of the hook so it is not masked thus reducing the chance of hooking fish. This is a much simplified version of the G. & H. sedge.

Hare's Ear Nymph, sizes 16-10 weighted and unweighted

Tail: Brown hackle fibres

Body: Fur from hare's poll

Rib: Gold wire

Wing Case: Hen pheasant tail

If this nymph is to be weighted, wind the desired amount of lead wire on to the hook being careful to leave enough room at the head end to tie off the wing case and form the head. As most mayfly nymphs are dark don't clip right down to the pale underfur on the hare's mask, use only the darker tips and paler guard hairs. Hatching nymphs have dark wing cases so there is a good case for tying some with black wing cases to imitate nymphs on their way to the surface.

Woolly Caddis, size 10 weighted

Body: Natural grey or brown wool over lead wire

I've tried several greyish brown shades of wool and there doesn't seem to be any difference in their fish catching ability. I wind the lead on in two or even two and a half layers. The half layer is just behind the eye of the hook so that when the wool is wound on the body tapers from front to back. Use heavy hooks. It isn't logical to wind lots of lead on a fine wire hook. This pattern should get caught up on the bottom occasionally if fished properly; a heavy hook helps it survive.

Midge Pupa, sizes 16-12

Body: Black floss

Rib: Silver wire or grey tying silk

Thorax: Grey ostrich herl or peacock herl

Breathing Filaments: White wool or white marabou

The body should extend round the bend of the hook. As this pattern is usually fished near the surface light hooks should be used.

No Hackle Dun, sizes 16-12

Tail: Two mink guard hairs or grizzle hackle fibres

Body: Various shades of grey polydub

Wing: Mallard primary feather or deer hair

Winging is the operation fly tyers find the most difficult. As these wings should be tied more on the side than on top of the hook it is easier to tie on one at a time. The tail is very important. It should be widely splayed, at least 90 degrees. To do this the first step is to dub on a tiny ball of the body material at the start of the bend of the hook. Tie in the tail fibres in front of this ball and it will keep them splayed out. The wings should be orientated so the natural curve of the feather is up and out.

If the deer hair wing version is preferred tie in a small bunch of deer hair, twenty or so fibres is enough and fan them out around the top of the hook shank. The deer hair model is more durable than the mallard quill version.

Pheasant Tail Nymph, sizes 16-14

Tail: Cock pheasant tail fibres

Body: Cock pheasant tail fibres

Wing Case: Cock pheasant tail fibres

No tying silk is used in the original Sawyer tie. Fine copper wire is used to tie in the fibres at the tail then wound forward to build up a thorax. The fibres are then wound forward, the wing case formed and tied off with the copper wire. If a lighter version is required substitute tying silk for the copper wire.

Spinner, sizes 16-14

Tail: Grizzle hackle fibres

Body: Cock pheasant tail

Hackle: Grizzle

I tie this one with a relatively small hackle and only a couple of turns of it. Again the tail is important, long fibres well splayed help flotation. The pheasant tail fibres are brittle and usually unwind after a fish or two, putting varnish on the hook shank and winding the fibres over it while still wet improves the durability.

Spent Spinner, sizes 16-14

Tail: Grizzle hackle fibres

Body: Cock pheasant tail

Wings: Grizzle hackle tips

The wings are tied spent and can be tied with the tips of the larger hackles of a grizzle cape that aren't much good for anything else. The wings should be about the same length as the body. If tied too long they tend to tangle in the bend of the hook.

EPILOGUE

Well that's it, ten tried and tested patterns. But remember, good flies are only part of the answer to the problem of catching fish. You need to know when to use them and I've given a few hints in that direction. You also need to be able to put them where you want them to be, quickly, without scaring the fish. The way to develop your skills is to get out and fish as often as possible, anywhere trout are to be caught. Tight lines and calm days!